MW01227838

The Playbook Kollection

Unite through Play, Learn through Activities!

The Playbook Kollection

Unite through Play, Learn through Activities!

By: Dr. Tonmar Johnson
&
Dr. Dewone Bennett

San Francisco

Grateful acknowledgement is given to all those who have paved the way for this adventure to begin. Love. Respect. Bravery. Truth. Honesty. Humility. Wisdom. Divine 9.

7th GAP Media
7thGAPMedia@gmail.com
Printed in the United States
Edited By: Ryan McMurray, M.S., Sociology
Contributions By: Marquel Johnson, MBA

1st edition: December 2024

Dedication

To all the young athletes who dream big and play with heart, this book is for you. May you always find happiness in the game and never stop chasing your goals. A special thanks to the coaches, parental figures, educators, and mentors who support and inspire the next generation of players. Your dedication and encouragement make all the difference.

ALSO AUTHORED BY DR. TONMAR JOHNSON

"Mysteries of a Middle Schooler" is an exciting adventure series filled with twists, challenges, and unforgettable discoveries.

Please visit **ReadMMS.com** for the exhilarating time traveling book anthology.

"Reading, of all kinds, is valuable for athletes because it strengthens the mind alongside the body. It also sharpens focus, eases stress, and builds mental resilience, which are all crucial for handling the pressures of competition. Reading also encourages strategic thinking, whether it is by learning from character association in books they enjoy, or from biographies of other athletes' experiences. It boosts communication skills, as well, which helps with team dynamics and post-game interviews. Most importantly, reading fosters a growth mindset, preparing athletes for life beyond sports and keeping them curious and open to new knowledge."

~Dr. T Johnson

Table of Contents

The PBK INTRODUCTION .... page 1

PSYCHOLOGICAL BENEFITS .... page 3

SOCIOLOGICAL BENEFITS .... page 4

GLOSSARY .... page 5

ELEMENTS of GOLF .... page 7

SCORING .... page 8

FUN FACT .... page 9

QUESTIONS to ASK .... page 11

RULES and GAMEPLAY .... page 12

COLORING SHEET .... page 14

OBJECTIVE and ETIQUETTE .... page 15

WORD SEARCH .... page 16

CROSSWORD PUZZLE .... page 17

FUN FACT .... page 18

MADLIB .... page 19

STRATEGIES and TIPS .... page 20

ART .... page 23

FUN FACT .... page 24

WRITING PROMPT .... page 25

WORD JUMBLE .... page 26

REVIEW .... page 27

NOTABLE RECORD HOLDERS .... page 28

NAME. IMAGE. LIKENESS. .... page 29

CONCLUSION ……………………………………… page 33

NOTES for PRACTICE …………………………… page 35

STRATEGIES ……………………………………… page 37

NOTES for DRILLS ……………………………… page 39

QUESTIONS ……………………………………… page 41

NOTE to SELF …………………………………… page 43

The PBK - Golf Edition

The Playbook Kollection is designed for all levels of athletes who are embarking on a voyage of discovery in sports. Throughout its pages, you will find a wide variety of information related to the sport you are looking to play. For educators and other forms of parental figures, there is information on the psychological and sociological benefits of playing team sports, along with some other key information that will help you facilitate a conversation with the child(ren). For kids, there are plenty of engaging activities to complete, as well as some information about the sport itself - for example, rules and gameplay, a glossary of terms, and some thought-provoking questions to ask yourself and or others.

This series aims to provide something for everyone. For the kids, The Playbook Kollection is packed with fun activities designed to help them learn the game in an interactive way. Coaches, educators, and parents will find detailed sections on how to encourage positive team dynamics and foster a supportive environment for young athletes. There are tips on how to handle the ups and downs of competitive sports, emphasizing the importance of resilience, teamwork, and communication.

As with any new adventure, questions are bound to arise along the way, particularly in the beginning of the journey. It is our hope that this book, and the others in the series, will serve as a go-to resource for any

1

questions you may have. Whether you are wondering about the best way to practice a particular skill, looking for advice on how to deal with game-day nerves, or simply curious about the history of the sport, the Playbook Series is here to help.

Happy reading from all of us at 7th Gap Media! We hope this series inspires a love of sports and helps you enjoy every step of your athletic journey. Be sure to explore our other books in The Playbook Kollection for guidance and tips on a variety of sports.

Psychological Benefits of Playing Team Sports

Starting to play a team sport comes with uncertainty for anyone, but the psychological benefits of playing team sports far outweigh any fear an individual may feel at the beginning. For example, a 2019 study by researchers at the Cleveland Clinic has shown that playing team sports can lead to significant improvements in overall concentration, enhanced communication skills, increased confidence levels, and improved sleeping habits (perfect for the individual who has trouble going to bed and/or falling asleep at night!) Additionally, when breaking down the study it also shows there is a decline in overall stress levels, depression, and anxiety which also come from playing team sports.

"Sport has provided a context where young people can feel empowered and successful." Dr. Dewone Bennett

Sociological Benefits of Playing Team Sports

From a sociological space the benefits of group activity, in an organized fashion, serve as a significant warning for youth who may look to other unhealthy options to active peer activity. Playing team sports offers kids a valuable experience in learning good teamwork skills, being part of a group that must communicate with one another to succeed, and the opportunity for social interaction and socialization. In addition, team sports will certainly create opportunities for youth to display good sportsmanship, and in healthy ways allow them to identify their strengths and weaknesses on and off of the field/court. Whether a game is won or lost, treating the other participants with respect and compassion is the mark of a "good sport."

"When examining the interests of the youth in any society, little is more appealing than sports." - Dr. Tonmar Johnson

4

Glossary

Backswing: The motion of the club moving away from the ball, setting up the golfer for the downswing and impact.

Ball marker: A small, flat object, sometimes a coin or a plastic disc, that is used to mark the position of a golfer's ball on the green while other players putt, or when the ball is lifted for cleaning.

Caddie: A person who assists a golfer during a round, carrying the golf bag, offering advice, and providing moral support.

Chip: A short, low-trajectory shot used to get the ball onto the green from a close distance, usually played with a wedge or short iron.

Club: The tool golfers use to hit the golf ball. There are several different kinds of clubs, including a driver, woods, irons, wedges, and putters. Each kind of club is designed for different situations you may encounter on the golf course.

Divot repair tool: A small tool used to repair ball marks on the green, ensuring a smooth surface for putting.

Fore: A warning shouted by golfers to alert others of an incoming ball that may hit them or come close.

Golf bag: A bag designed to organize and carry clubs and other golf accessories, such as balls, tees, and gloves.

Golf glove: A protective covering worn on the lead hand (the left hand for right-handed golfers) to improve grip and prevent blisters.

Golf shoes: Shoes with spikes or molded grips on the sole for improved traction on the course.

Golf umbrella: A large umbrella designed to protect golfers and their equipment from rain or sun on the course.

Grip: The way a golfer holds the club, affecting control, power, and shot shape.

Honors: The privilege of teeing off first, typically awarded to the golfer with the lowest score on the previous hole.

Irons: A set of clubs with a flat, angled face used for various shots, numbered from 3-9, with higher numbers indicating a higher loft and shorter distance.

Mulligan: An informal term for retaking a shot without penalty, typically allowed only in casual rounds among friends.

Putter: A club designed specifically for putting, with a flat-faced head used to roll the ball along the green.

Shank: A severe mishit where the ball contacts the club's hosel, causing it to veer sharply to the right (for a right-handed golfer).

Slice: A shot that curves significantly from left to right (for a right-handed golfer), typically caused by an open clubface at impact.

Swing plane: The imaginary, tilted surface that the club travels on during the backswing and downswing, affecting the shot's accuracy and consistency.

Tee: A small wooden or plastic peg that is stuck in the ground to elevate the ball for the first shot on each hole.

Woods: A set of clubs with a rounded head used for long-distance shots.

Wedges: A type of iron club designed for short-range shots and specialty situations, such as escaping from bunkers.

Yardage markers: Colored markers or plates on the course that indicate distances to the green, usually measured in yards.

Elements of a Golf Course

Hole: A small, circular hole in the ground on the green, into which players aim to get the ball in as few shots as possible.

Tee box: The area where players "tee off" on each hole. "Tee off" is another term for a player's first shot.

Fairway: The short grassy area between the tee box and the green, where most play occurs.

Rough: The taller grass areas surrounding the fairway and green. Shooting from the rough is more difficult due to reduced ball visibility and control.

Green: The smooth, very short grass area surrounding the hole

Bunker: A sand-filled depression on the course, designed as an obstacle to make play more challenging. Bunkers can also be called "sand traps."

Water hazard: Any body of water on the course, such as lakes or streams, that also serve as obstacles.

Out of bounds: The area beyond the course's designated boundaries, usually marked by white stakes, where play is prohibited.

Pin/flag: A tall pole with a flag, inserted into the hole to show players its location on the green.

Hazard: Any obstacle on the course, such as bunkers, water, or thick rough, designed to challenge players and add difficulty to shots.

Cart path: A designated path for golf carts to travel on, minimizing wear and tear on the course.

Scoring

Hole-in-one: A player gets the ball into the hole with a single shot, typically on a par-3 hole.

Par: The standard number of strokes assigned to a hole or course, representing the expected score for a skilled golfer. For example, if a hole is rated at "par 4," this means that a skilled golfer should be able to put the ball into the hole in 4 shots.

Birdie: A score of one stroke less than par on a hole. For example, if a player gets the ball into the hole in 3 strokes on a par 4 hole, they have scored a birdie.

Eagle: A score of two strokes less than par on a hole.

Match play: A format in which golfers compete hole by hole, with the winner of each hole earning a point.

Bogey: A score of one stroke more than par on a hole.

Double bogey: A score of two strokes more than par on a hole.

Handicap: A numerical representation of a golfer's playing ability, allowing players of different skill levels to compete fairly against each other.

Net score: The golfer's gross score adjusted for their handicap, representing their actual performance relative to their skill level.

Are there any other terms and definitions you would like to add

Golf Fun Fact!

The modern game of golf can be traced back to
a game played on the eastern coast of
Scotland several centuries ago. In the earliest
version of the game, players would attempt to
hit a pebble over sand dunes and around

tracks with a bent stick or club. Eventually, the
rules of the game were written down in 1744.
Since that time, the game has continued to
change and evolve into the game we know
today.

Now it's your turn. Write a fun fact that you might know or have
Googled about the game of golf!

_____

_____

_____

_____

_____

_____

_____

Questions to Ask Your Teacher, Coach, and Parental Figure(s)

Record your answers below!

1. What sport(s) did you play when you were my age?

2. What was your favorite position and what positions did you play?

3. What was your favorite thing about playing sports?

4. How did you deal with tough losses? What about great wins?

5. How often did you practice per week?

Rules and Gameplay

The field of play for a game of golf is called the **course**, which is divided into eighteen holes (or 9 holes for a shortened game). Golf courses are extremely large places - a single hole can take up hundreds of yards worth of space!

Players start from the **tee box** to take their first shot, also called a **stroke**, and hit the ball towards the hole. Because the hole is so far away from the tee box, there is a long pole and a brightly colored flag stuck into the hole, so that players can see where it is from the tee box.

Each player takes their shot in turns, and play continues until every player has gotten their ball into the hole. Players keep their own scores, marking a single point for every stroke they take. At the end of the game, the player with the fewest strokes (or the lowest score) is the winner. This scoring style is different from many other sports, in which the team or player with the highest score is the winner.

Sometimes, though, a player will hit their ball into a place where it is difficult (or even impossible) to hit the ball towards the hole (for example, into the woods, or into a lake). The rules of golf state that a player may not move obstacles such as branches, twigs, sand, etc. out of the way to take their shot. If a player thinks that they cannot make a good shot because of these obstacles, they can choose to take a one-stroke penalty, move their ball a distance away, and take their next shot from a better place on the course.

If a player loses their ball after a stroke, they are given three minutes to find it. If they cannot find their ball, they are given a one-stroke penalty, and play continues.

Each hole on a golf course has a **par rating**. This is the number of strokes a skilled golfer would take to get their ball into the hole. So, for example, a **par-4** hole means It would take a skilled golfer 4 strokes to reach the hole. Players count their shots for each hole, and if they take more shots than the par rating to reach the hole, they are said to be **over par**. If they take fewer shots than the par rating, they are **under par**. At the end of the game, the player who has the greatest number of shots under par is the winner (or, if no player is under par, the player with the lowest number of total strokes is the winner).

Coloring Page!

Color in this golf scene in any way you like!

Objective and Etiquette

The object of golf as a game is to play the ball from the teeing into the hole on the green in as few strokes as possible, while also understanding the rules and the course's layout. The overall intention is to complete the course, which normally consists of 18 holes, with the fewest number of total strokes. Golfers compete either against each other or against the course itself, in different formats such as stroke play, match play, or various team competitions.

Golf is a sport rich in tradition and players are expected to play the ball as it lies, repair divots, rake bunkers, and generally ensure they leave the course in good condition for others.

Etiquette: pace of play, proper language, safety for other players, dress codes.

Honesty: following the rules, marking the ball properly, keeping an accurate score.

Respect: courtesy, provide assistance for lost balls, do not walk near or talk during a players stoke/putt.

Word Search!

Find all the words listed in the word bank. Words can be horizontal, vertical, diagonal, or even backwards! Good luck!

```
J  B  H  B  U  N  K  E  R  H  J  E  Y  Q  U
P  G  F  C  J  E  P  D  Z  S  Q  L  Y  D  Y
P  V  A  P  Q  K  W  H  U  E  D  G  J  X  C
D  G  I  V  S  Y  I  J  I  R  L  A  E  E  T
Q  L  R  P  F  P  E  D  I  F  H  E  L  M  Q
G  T  W  U  S  K  R  V  I  B  Q  X  L  N  W
G  P  A  T  J  I  E  A  T  W  F  P  C  T  S
E  R  Y  T  B  R  Y  O  G  X  K  B  H  A  Q
W  Y  E  O  F  W  R  A  E  A  H  Z  E  L  K
K  R  H  E  I  N  A  D  Z  N  L  L  Q  M  H
R  A  N  N  N  R  R  R  K  L  N  F  N  I  A
W  S  G  N  G  P  O  Y  E  G  O  B  R  U  V
M  U  Q  W  G  U  X  C  S  N  O  U  O  O  N
V  S  N  V  G  C  F  Z  Z  H  N  R  R  H  Y
I  M  D  H  W  E  S  G  W  P  D  P  R  L  G
```

Word Bank

Birdie	Driver	Flag	Rough
Eagle	Green	Bogey	Bunker
Fairway	Putt	Tee	PB (playbook)

16

Crossword Puzzle!

Use the clues provided to fill in the puzzle below. Words can go across or down and intersect where two words share a letter.

ACROSS

2. each hole has one of these, so that golfers can see where the hole is from far away
4. a score of one stroke more than par for any given hole
5. an area filled with sand or dirt on the golf course
6. a type of golf club used for shots on the green, close to the hole

DOWN

1. a score of two less than par for any given hole
3. an area of very short grass that contains each hole
4. a score of one less than par for any given hole
6. the number of strokes a skilled golfer would take to get their ball into each hole on a golf course
7. the small wooden peg golfers set their ball on for the first stroke

Golf Fun Fact!

In addition to being the second-ever Black student at Harvard University, George Franklin Grant (1846-1910) also loved the game of golf. In fact, Mr. Grant loved golf so much he had a course built on his home property, and was also the inventor of the golf tee, originally made from wood and rubber. Mr. Grant was awarded a US Patent for his invention in 1899.

Mad Libs!

Fill in the blanks as a friend reads the missing parts of speech to you. Then, read the finished story aloud to see how it turns out!

This weekend, my (1) _____ and I are going to the golf

(2) _____! We're all (3) _____ to play a round

and see who (4) _____. (5) _____ says

that she'll probably win, but (6) _____ says that he'll

win because he has more (7) _____ playing golf. My

(8) _____ got me a (9) _____ set of clubs for

my birthday, and I can't wait to (10) _____ them

out! They're just the right length and weight for me, and they're so

(11) _____. Even though this will be my first time

(12) _____ golf on a real (13) _____,

I'm more excited than (14) _____. To get ready for this

weekend, I've been watching videos of (15) _____

online. I know it will take a lot of (16) _____ to

become as good at golf as them, but I (17) _____ I can

do it if I try!

Parts of Speech Key

1: plural noun	2: noun	3: adjective
4: verb ending in "s"	5: friend's name	6: second friend's name
7: noun	8: plural noun	9: adjective
10: verb	11: adjective	12: verb ending in "ing"
13: noun	14: adjective	15: golf star's name
16: noun	17: verb	

Strategies and Tips

Dealing with game-day nerves is a common challenge for athletes of all skill levels, but there are several effective strategies to manage and overcome them:

Mental Strategies

1. Visualization: Imagine yourself performing well in the game. Visualizing success can help build confidence and reduce anxiety.
2. Positive Self-Talk: Replace negative thoughts with positive affirmations. Remind yourself of past successes and your strengths.
3. Focus on the Process: Concentrate on what you need to do moment by moment rather than the outcome of the game.
4. Mindfulness and Meditation: Practice mindfulness or meditation techniques to stay present and calm your mind.

Physical Strategies

1. Breathing Exercises: Practice deep, controlled breathing to reduce physical symptoms of anxiety. Techniques like box breathing (inhaling for four counts, holding for four, exhaling for four, holding for four) can be effective.
2. Progressive Muscle Relaxation: Tense and then relax each muscle group in your body to release tension.
3. Pre-Game Routine / Warm Up: Establish a consistent pre-game routine to create a sense of normalcy and control.
4. Warm-Up Properly: Ensure a thorough warm-up to get your body ready and reduce nervous energy.

Supportive Strategies

1. Talk to Someone: Share your feelings with a parental figure, family member, coach, teammate, or mentor who can provide reassurance and advice.
2. Team Bonding: Strengthening relationships with teammates can create a supportive environment that alleviates pressure.
3. Laugh and Have Fun: Humor and light-hearted interactions can diffuse tension and remind you to enjoy the game.

Behavioral Strategies

1. Preparation: Be well-prepared for the game by practicing and knowing your role. Confidence in your abilities can significantly reduce nerves.
2. Set Small Goals: Focus on achieving small, manageable goals during the game rather than the overall result.
3. Stay Engaged: Keep yourself engaged with your team and the game plan. Distraction from nervous thoughts can help keep anxiety at bay.
4. Rituals and Superstitions: If you have a lucky charm or a pre-game ritual, it can provide comfort and reduce anxiety.

Professional Help

1. Sports Psychologist/ Counselor: Think about working with someone who can offer specialized strategies and support for your overall mental health.

***For more information feel free to contact a specialist at DBennettCounseling.com

Practical Tips

1. Healthy Lifestyle: Ensure you're getting enough sleep, eating well, and staying hydrated, as physical well-being impacts mental state.
2. Music: Listen to calming or motivating music before the game to shift your mood.
3. Control What You Can: Focus on factors within your control, such as effort and attitude, rather than the unpredictable elements of the game.

Post-Game Reflection

1. Reflect Positively: After the game, reflect on what went well and what you can improve, maintaining a positive outlook on your progress.
2. Learn from Experience: Use each game as a learning experience to better handle nerves in the future.

***By mixing in these strategies into your routine, any athlete can manage game-day nerves more effectively and perform at their best.

Art Prompt

Draw a challenging golf hole! Feel free to add obstacles such as bunkers, water hazards, and rough wherever you like. Now describe your drawing

_____

_____

_____

_____

Color, hashtag (#TPS), tag (ThePlaybookKollection), and post for a chance to win a prize.

Golf Fun Fact!

When golf was first invented, only men were allowed to play, but advances for women's rights in the 19th century changed that. The first recorded game of women's golf was played in Musselburgh, Scotland in 1867. Shortly after that, women's golf clubs and golf leagues began to spring up. Today, professional golf in most countries have both a men's league (the Professional Golfer's Association, or PGA) and a women's league (the Ladies Professional Golf Association, or LPGA).

Writing Prompt

What do you think is the most exciting, and challenging thing about playing golf? Why do you play golf and what do you hope to gain from the sport? Who is your current or former favorite player?

_____

_____

_____

_____

_____

_____

_____

_____

_____

_____

_____

_____

Word Jumble!

Unscramble the words on the left and write them in the spaces provided.

RVDIRE   __ __ __ __ __ __

GLAEE   __ __ __ __ __

GRUHO   __ __ __ __ __

KRUNBE   __ __ __ __ __ __

UTP   __ __ __

GYBEO   __ __ __ __ __

YRFAWYI   __ __ __ __ __ __

RNOI   __ __ __ __

DGEWE   __ __ __ __ __

PREUTT   __ __ __ __ __ __

RDUEN ARP   __ __ __ __ __   __ __ __

Let's Review What We've Learned!

Below is a short quiz to review and recap what you've learned. Fill in your answers and have a parent or coach check them!

1. Golfers stand in the _____ to take their first shot.

2. Which of these is another name for a bunker?

   a. Sand dune   b. Dirt patch
   c. Sand trap   d. Grit hazard

3. True/False: A score of two over par on any golf

   hole is called a **double bogey**.

4. If your ball is stuck in a bunker, the best type of

   club to use is a _____.

5. Putters are mainly used on the _____.

6. When in need of help with strategies and tips, you

   should look to which of these?

   a. Coaches   b. Parental figure
   c. Teachers   d. Any of the above

Notable Records in Professional Golf

Tiger Woods holds the record for the most consecutive weeks as the world's #1 professional golfer at **683** weeks!

Lydia Ko won a record **10 LPGA Tour** victories before turning 19 years old!

Kathy Whitworth won a record **88 LPGA Tournaments** and **Tour Player of the Year:** 1966, 1967, 1968, 1969, 1971, 1972, 1973!

Phil Mickelson spent a record **26 years** on the top 50 Golfers List!

In 1964, Althea Gibson reigned as the very first African American woman to play on the LPGA Tour. She was also an American tennis player and in 1956, she became the first African American to win a Grand Slam event.

In 1998, **Annika Sorenstam** was the first LPGA player to hold a scoring average under 70!

From a span from 1948 to 1962, **Patty Berg** won 44 professional titles and three **Vare Trophies**. By the end of her career, she was credited with **60** professional victories with **15** major championships, including the 1946 U.S. Women's Open Championship.

Jack Nicklaus holds the most titles at **18 PGA** Major Tournament!

Name. Image. Likeness

What is N.I.L.?

As of June 2021, all eligible college athletes can now receive financial compensation for their name, image, and likeness through marketing and promotional opportunities. Today's collegiate athletes are getting paid through endorsements, sponsorships, and commercial opportunities using their name, image, and likeness.

N.I.L. History

Before 2021, receiving money as a college athlete was restricted by NCAA rules and considered illegal. Athletes were not allowed to receive any financial benefits from their name, image, and likeness as collegiate athletes. Many former players who received money and were caught have had their awards taken from them. A popular household name, Reggie Bush, is a prime example of an athlete who was compensated in secret. Bush was ultimately punished for violating NCAA rules. There is now an argument circulating in the industry that players who received financial compensation in the past and were caught should now be compensated and re-awarded their honors.

How is N.I.L. beneficial?

Name, image, and likeness deals can be beneficial because they provide college athletes with opportunities to profit from their name, image, and likeness. Colleges have forever profited off athletes' names, images, and likenesses without providing compensation in forms other than scholarships. According to ESPN, with NIL allowing student-athletes to earn money while in college, more student-athletes have chosen to continue their education and finish their degrees.

How to get access to an N.I.L.?

To obtain access to a NIL deal, athletes and parents must familiarize themselves with the NIL rules, build a brand, develop a social media presence, network with brands and agencies, focus on authentic partnerships, remain professional, and in certain cases seek legal guidance. Following these steps and actively working to build a personal brand and network is an essential component of nailing a deal. As an athlete, build your brand around what makes you the athlete you are. If your nutrition and workout routine is a key factor in your high performance, document and post your meal plan and workout routine throughout the weeks. Developing a brand with a purpose tailored to your talents and interests is how to attract partnerships with companies aligned with your personal brand as an athlete.

Is N.I.L. money taxable?

Understanding the tax side of an NIL deal is very critical. Endorsements, sponsorships, content creation, guest appearances, and merchandise are all considered taxable earnings. Understanding how often you will be getting paid will determine how often you pay taxes on the income you receive. For example, if you are asked to fill out a W-4, you are most likely considered an employee, and your employer takes taxes out each payment.

However, if you are asked to fill out a W-9, you are considered self-employed and must send quarterly tax payments on your own. It is also important to consider how much you will make vs the support you receive from your parents because your income can affect whether your parents can claim you on their taxes or not. If you make too much through deals, you will not be able to file with your parents. Also, make sure you are keeping track of the states you work in. You may need to file taxes in different states depending on where you have worked. Lastly, your NIL money affects your financial aid status and possibly scholarships. Depending on what you make, you may no longer qualify for regular need-based scholarships and must pay for school out of your earnings. Therefore, it is important to consider the financial aspects of the NIL deal and determine if it works for you and your goals.

References

H&R Block. (2024). NIL student athlete checklist.https://www.hrblock.com/tax-center/income/nil-athlete-tax-checklist/

Conclusion

We hope you've had a great time learning about the game of golf! Starting any new activity usually comes with some challenges, especially in the beginning. However, as you continue to practice and play matches with and against your friends, you'll find that things will get easier. Starting any new sport will also take a lot of energy, so be sure to drink a lot of water and stretch your muscles both before and after practice, scrimmages, or games. Overall though, make sure to try your best (and we know you will), and have fun playing. Remember, golf is not just about individual skills but also about teamwork, strategy, and sportsmanship. As you develop your abilities, pay attention to how you can contribute and support your fellow golfers. Celebrate your victories, learn from your defeats, and always keep a positive attitude.

If you ever feel frustrated, remember that every great player once started where you are now. Persistence and a positive mindset are key to improving your game.

Best of luck on your golf journey from all of us here at 7th Gap Media! Please check out the rest of The Playbook Kollection material for any of your sport's needs. Whether you're interested in basketball, softball, football, pickleball, track & field, soccer or any other sport, we've got you covered with tips, strategies, and inspiration to help you succeed and enjoy the game.

~The Playbook

Notes for Practice

Strategies

Notes for Drills

Questions

Notes to Self

Made in the USA
Columbia, SC
04 December 2024

47583222R00031